SONGS & RHYMES
for transition times

150 TRANSITIONS for the PRESCHOOL CLASSROOM

ANGELA THAYER

Songs and Rhymes for Transition Times: 150 Transitions for the Preschool Classroom

All contents copyright © 2017 by Angela Thayer

TeachingMama.org

All rights reserved.

This book is for personal or classroom use. By using it, you agree to not to copy and distribute the contents, except for your own personal, non-commercial use.

Publishing and Design Services: MartinPublishingServices.com

Clipart: Laura Strickland of WhimsyClips.com

Table of Contents

Introduction 1

Planning Transitions 4

Beginning the Day 5

Circle Time 15

Attention-Getters 23

Handwashing 29

Lining Up 39

Outside 49

Cleaning Up 59

Brain Breaks 69

    Action Breaks 70

    Crossing the Midline 79

    Finger Plays 86

Building Character 95

End of Day 103

About the Author 112

"If everyone started off the day singing, just think how happy they'd be."

– Lauren Myracle

Introduction

Numerous times throughout the day in a preschool classroom, children move from one activity to another. For some students, this is an easy task. For others, transition times add confusion, challenges, and frustration to their day. As educators, we want the best for our students and we want to see them succeed in school. Learning how to transition efficiently between activities leads to more time for children to be engaged in learning activities and fewer behavior problems in the classroom.

This book is all about music transitions and how to incorporate them into your preschool day. There are many types of transitions to use in a classroom, but this book will focus on the use of songs, chants, and rhymes.

Have you ever noticed that when it's time to line up for the hallway or clean up, students begin to act out? When there is less structure, children know that your attention is not completely on them. This is exactly why you need to add transitions into your day! I like to think of transitions as special tricks to help your day run more smoothly. It adds structure to times when students tend to misbehave. Having a plan for what transitions you'll use during the day is vital and it will give you better classroom management skills.

There are 5 key benefits for using transitions in your preschool classroom:

Classroom Community

Music Skills

Routine

Physical Skills

Brain Breaks

Introduction

CLASSROOM COMMUNITY

Using transitions in your day encourages social cohesion for your classroom. This helps students feel a sense of belonging at school. It's important for children to have a positive outlook about school and themselves. Group activities, like transitions, can help promote a positive attitude toward school.

MUSIC SKILLS

Have you ever noticed how music has the ability to calm an anxious child, grab the attention of a lively group, and make children happy? Music is so powerful! Singing songs increases positive attitudes and is also a stress reducer. While singing, children also can learn rhythm, rhyming, and how to use their singing voice. We don't have to be trained singers to add music to our classroom. Children don't care if you're a little off pitch or don't sing the song perfectly. They just love music!

ROUTINE

Children thrive with routines and schedules. Furthermore, our brains love patterns because it helps us connect and understand what will happen next. When classrooms have routines, the number of behavior problems is reduced. Routines help children understand the expectations of the environment.

PHYSICAL SKILLS

Using transitions with movement enhances physical skill development. Hopping, skipping, jumping, and dancing are not only fun for kids, but also great for exercise and developing motor skills. Using movement with transition songs and chants stimulates the brain and energizes our bodies!

BRAIN BREAKS

It is very important to add brain breaks into your day! These breaks are used to activate and stimulate a child's brain. They also improve a child's ability to concentrate and are a wonderful way to relieve stress. Did you know research found that children should have a kinesthetic brain break every 25-30 minutes? These do not have to be long breaks, but they go a long way in helping a child succeed in the classroom.

Songs and Rhymes for Transition Times will cover a variety of music transitions to help you create the amazing classroom environment you've always dreamed of. This isn't a book filled with sheet music, but instead it is a book of songs set to familiar tunes, rhythmic chants, and rhymes. I promise you that using just a handful of these transitions will help your day run more smoothly and will bring more peace to your classroom.

"It's the teacher that makes the difference, not the classroom."

– Michael Morpurgo

Planning Transitions

One of the challenges as a teacher is knowing how to plan transitions into your day. You may wonder what time of day to use them or how many of them you should schedule into your day. Timing should always be considered when planning transitions. Challenging behavior is more likely to happen when there are too many transitions in the day, the transition time is too long, or when children are not clear on the directions.

I encourage you to look at your schedule and think about the times when you expect behavior problems to arise or times you know the schedule is more unstructured. For example, you may want to add in a brain break when you know students need to get up and move around. You may also want to plan for a calm transition song when you are gathering for circle time.

This book contains 150 songs, rhymes, and chants for these 10 categories:

- Beginning of the Day
- Circle Time
- Attention-Getters
- Handwashing
- Lining Up and Hallway
- Cleaning Up
- Outside Time
- Brain Breaks: Action Breaks, Crossing the Midline, Finger Plays
- Building Character
- End of Day

Once you've decided which transitions to use, you will need to teach your students the expectations and steps. It's important to model this multiple times in multiple ways. One way to do this is by role-playing with the students. Students love to see you role-play with the opposite behavior to show students what they should not do. Another way to do this is by adding visual cues. Display a poster of the handwashing guidelines or have picture cards that show the order of the schedule for the day.

As you teach transitions to your students, make sure to praise children when they practice them well. Remember that children learn differently and you may have to teach these expectations in a variety of ways.

Transitions are powerful and will help both beginning and seasoned teachers create a more peaceful environment for students.

Beginning the Day

The beginning of the day is the perfect time to welcome students to your classroom and remind them of the friendly environment they come to each day. Some of these songs focus on learning students' names and others are just great for greeting one another. Starting the day with a cheerful song is a great way to set the tone for the day.

Beginning the Day

Do You Know What Time It Is?

Tune: The Muffin Man

Do you know what time it is?
What time it is, what time it is?
Do you know what time it is?
It's time to start our day!

Hey, Hey! It's Time to Start Our Day!

Chant

Hey, hey! What do you say?
It's time for us to start our day!
Grab a friend's hand and shake hello!
Tell them something fun you know!
Find your seat and look around.
It's time to start, so sit right down!

Beginning the Day

Clap a Friend's Name

Tune: London Bridge Is Falling Down

Clap a friend's name with me,
Name with me, name with me.
Clap a friend's name with me,
Let's clap *(name)*.

Variations: snap, stomp, pat, skip

Hello, Neighbor!

Chant

Hello, neighbor! *(wave)*
What do you say? *(shake hands)*
It's going to be a beautiful day!
(make a circle with both hands in front of you)
So clap your hands, *(clap hands)*
And stomp your feet. *(stomp feet)*
Jump up and down *(jump)*
And have a seat! *(sit down)*

Beginning the Day

What Color Are You Wearing?

Tune: Mary Had a Little Lamb

If you're wearing red today,
Red today, red today –
If you're wearing red today,
Stand up and shout "hooray!"

(Repeat the song and change the color.)

Good Morning, Preschool Friends

Tune: If You're Happy and You Know It

Good morning, preschool friends,
How are you? *(arms in the air pumping, saying "good, good!")*
Good morning, preschool friends,
How are you? *(arms in the air pumping, saying "good, good!")*
It's time to start our day,
We are here to work and play.
Good morning, preschool friends,
How are you? *(arms in the air pumping, saying "good, good!")*

Hello, Afternoon Friends

Tune: If You're Happy and You Know It

Hello, afternoon friends,
How are you? *(arms in the air pumping, saying "good, good!")*
Hello, afternoon friends,
How are you? *(arms in the air pumping, saying "good, good!")*
It's time to start our day
We are here to work and play.
Hello, afternoon friends,
How are you? *(arms in the air pumping saying "good, good!")*

It's Time to Start Our Day

Tune: The Farmer in the Dell

It's time to start our day.
It's time to start our day.
It's time to give a great big cheer
'Cause learning time is near!
Hooray!

Beginning the Day

Ready for the Day

Tune: If You're Happy and You Know It

If you're ready for the day, find your seat. *(clap, clap)*
If you're ready for the day, find your seat. *(clap, clap)*
Check your hands, check your feet,
If you're ready, find your seat.
If you're ready for the day, find your seat. *(clap, clap)*

I See Friends Looking at Me!

Chant: Brown Bear, Brown Bear

(child's name, child's name) who do you see?
I see *(child's name)* looking at me!

*(Continue this chant around the room
until everyone has been named.)*

Beginning the Day

Wiggle Your Fingers, Stomp Your Feet!

Chant

Wiggle your fingers in the air.
Wiggle them, wiggle them everywhere!
Stomp your feet upon the ground.
Stomp them, stomp them all around.
Now sit down and cross your feet.
Hands in lap, nice and neat.
Now we are ready to start our day,
We'll listen first, and then we'll play.

Our Friends' Names

Tune: Are You Sleeping?

Say a friend's name,
Say a friend's name,
After me,
After me.
Saying names is so much fun,
Especially this one,
(child's name),
(child's name).

Beginning the Day

Wave Hello!

Tune: Wheels on the Bus

Hey everybody wave hello,
Wave hello, wave hello.
Hey everybody wave hello,
And say good morning to *(child's name)*.

Where Is _____?

Tune: Are You Sleeping?

Where is *(child's name)*?
Where is *(child's name)*?
Here I am. *(child sings)*
Here I am. *(child sings)*
We're so glad to see you,
We're so glad to see you,
At our school,
At our school.

Beginning the Day

Let's Start Our Day

Chant

Hey, hey friends!
Let's start on our day!
But first let's make some monkey sounds!
Ooh Ooh, Ahh Ahh!
Ooh Ooh, Ahh Ahh!

Hey, hey friends!
Let's start on our day!
But first let's make some chicken sounds!
Cluck, cluck, cluck!
Cluck, cluck, cluck!

Hey, hey friends!
Let's start on our day!
But first let's make some owl sounds!
Hoot, hoot, hoot!
Hoot, hoot, hoot!

Hey, hey friends!
Let's start on our day!
But first let's make some kitty cat sounds!
Meow, meow, meow!
Meow, meow, meow!

Circle Time

It can be hard to get students to focus during circle time. There are times when you need their attention to come to the group or times when you need to remind students how to act when they are sitting in a group. These 10 songs will help with that!

Coming to Group

Listen and Do

Chant

1, 2, listen and do.
3, 4, meet at the floor.
5, 6, silent lips.
7, 8, don't be late!
9, 10 we're ready again!

Circle Time

Meet at the Rug

Chant

Snap, crackle, pop!
It's time for us to stop!
Meet me at the rug.
Let's all get comfy and snug!

Circle Time

Tune: O' Christmas Tree

Oh circle time, oh circle time!
It's time for us to meet.
Oh circle time, oh circle time!
It's time for us to meet.
Gather on the rug right now,
Our preschool friends can show us how.
Oh circle time, oh circle time!
It's time for us to meet.

Circle Time

Come to Group

Tune: Mary Had a Little Lamb

If you hear me come to group,
Come to group, come to group.
If you hear me, come to group.
It's time for learning!

Listen Up!

Tune: Jingle Bells

Listen up, Listen up!
It's time for circle time.
Make your way down to the floor,
It's time to learn some more!

Circle Time

At Group

Wiggle Chant

Chant

Get your wiggles out.
Let's wiggle, wiggle, wiggle!
(wiggle your body)
Pull your wiggle out and throw it like a ball.
(pretend to throw a ball)
Now your wiggle's gone and
it's bouncing down the hall!

Circle Time

How We Sit Song

Tune: Here We Go 'Round the Mulberry Bush

This is the way we cross our legs,
Cross our legs, cross our legs.
This is the way we cross our legs, when it's circle time.
This is the way we fold our hands,
Fold our hands, fold our hands.
This is the way we fold our hands, when it's circle time.
This is the way we zip our lips,
Zip our lips, zip our lips.
This is the way we zip our lips, when it's circle time.

Criss Cross Applesauce

Chant

Criss cross applesauce,
Hands on lap, gingersnap.
Back straight, chocolate shake.
On my rear, root beer.
Lips zipped, cool whip.
Shhhhh!

Circle Time

Let's Get Ready!

Chant

Wiggle your fingers. *(wiggle fingers)*
Wiggle your toes. *(wiggle toes)*
Wiggle your ears. *(move ear lobes back and forth)*
Wiggle your nose. *(wiggle nose with your fingers)*
Now that we've had our fill,
It's time for us to sit still. *(fold hands in your lap)*

Criss Cross, Zip Your Lips

Chant

Criss, criss, cross!
Criss, cross applesauce! *(cross your legs and sit)*
Zip, zip, zip!
We zip our lips so quick! *(zipping motion on lips)*

Attention-Getters

Attention-getters are chants to get the attention of your class. This may be at a time when they are getting too noisy or you want to stop the class to give students directions. Clapping patterns, turning off the lights, or using a bell are a few ways to get the attention of your class. Here are 10 transitions to use as attention-getters.

Attention-Getters

5 Clap Chant

Chant

(clap, clap...clap, clap, clap)
Listen. Listen up!
(clap, clap...clap, clap, clap)
It's time to...time to stop!

Facing Me

Tune: Head, Shoulders, Knees, and Toes

Eyes and bodies facing me, facing me.
Eyes and bodies facing me, facing me.
Time to stop and listen, 1, 2, 3!
Eyes and bodies facing me, facing me.

Attention-Getters

Clapping Patterns Chant

Chant

If you can hear my voice, clap once. *(clap)*
If you can hear my voice, clap twice. *(clap, clap)*
If you can hear my voice, clap three times
(clap, clap, clap) and find your seat.

(You can change this up to do different clapping patterns and to signal to your students what you want them to do.)

(You can start with a whisper and grow to a louder voice.)

Train Chant

Chant

Chugga chugga, *(teacher)*
Choo choo! *(students)*
It's time for you to listen and do! *(teacher)*

Attention-Getters

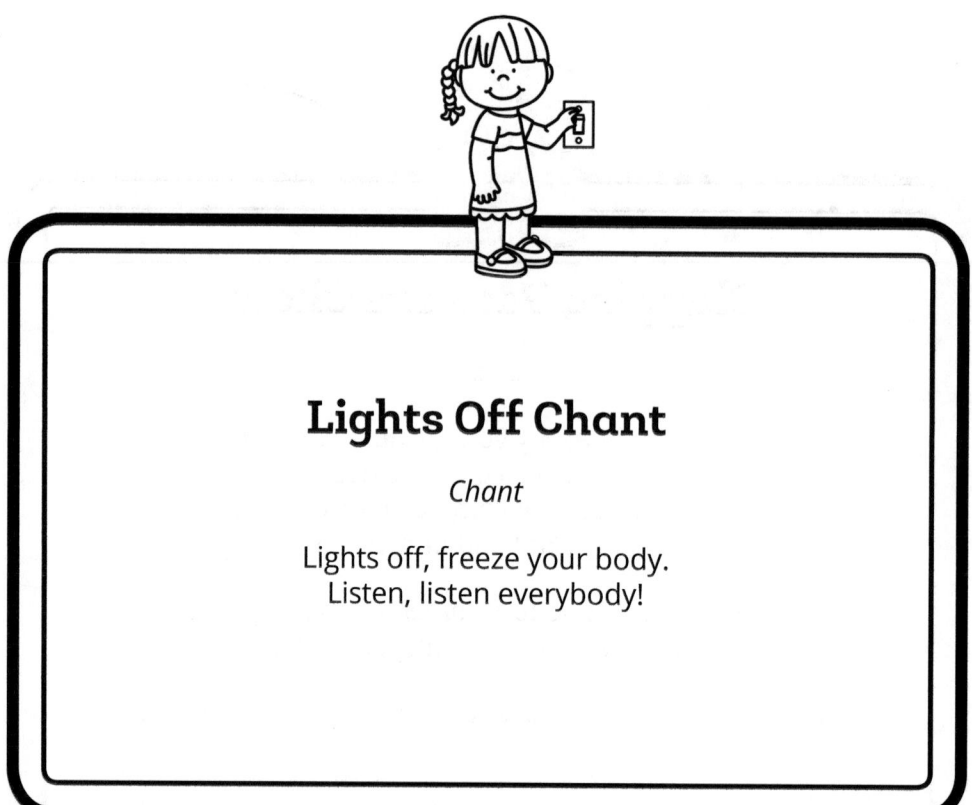

Lights Off Chant

Chant

Lights off, freeze your body.
Listen, listen everybody!

Freeze Chant

Chant

Snap, snap, snap, snap.
Snap your fingers, now let's clap.

Clap, clap, clap, clap.
Clap your hands, and now let's stomp.

Stomp, stomp, stomp, stomp.
Stomp your feet, and now let's freeze!

Attention-Getters

Yippie Yi Yay!

Chant

Yippie Yi Yay!
It's time to look this way!
Yippie Yi Yay!
Let's make it a good day!

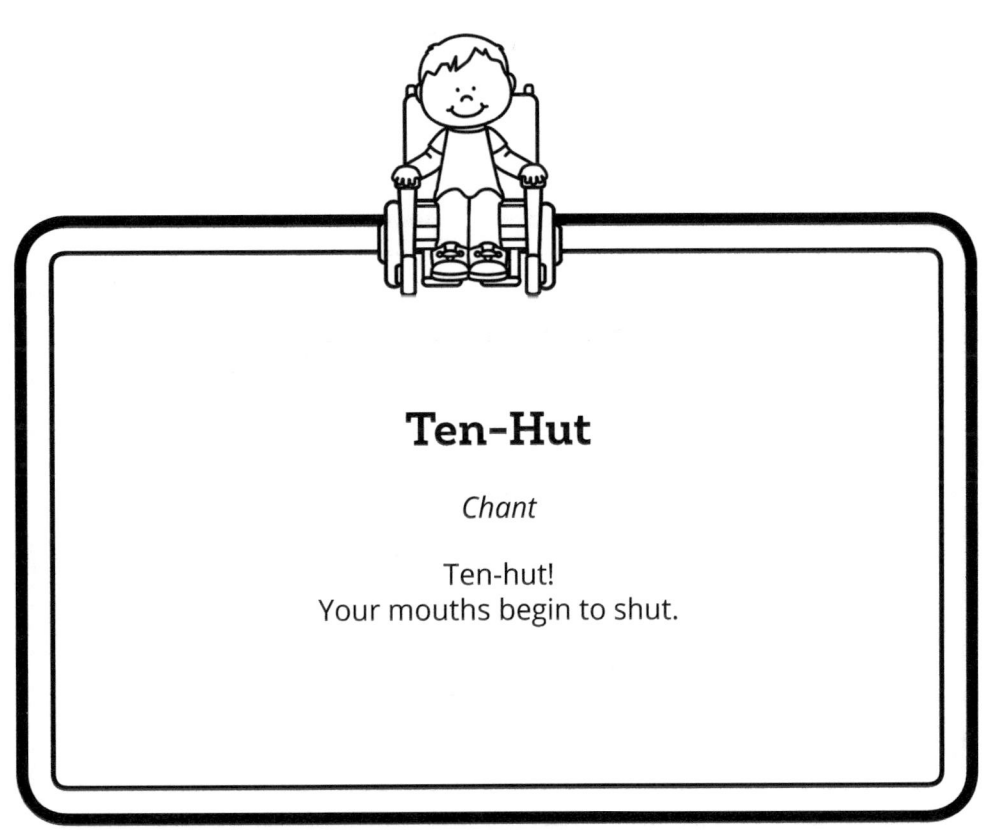

Ten-Hut

Chant

Ten-hut!
Your mouths begin to shut.

Attention-Getters

Look, Listen, Stop!

Chant

Clap, clap, clap.
Look, listen, stop!
Clap, clap, clap.
Your voices should be stopped.

Zip A Dee Do Dah Listening Song

Tune: Zip A Dee Do Dah

Zip A Dee Do Dah,
Zip A Dee Ay!
Lots of learning is happening today!
Look at the teacher,
Hear what he/she says.
Zip A Dee Do Dah,
Zip A Dee Ay!

Handwashing

Singing a tune while washing hands helps children remember the directions and also helps them wash their hands long enough. Many children forget to wash their hands for the recommended twenty seconds, so singing a song is a good way to help them measure if they have been scrubbing long enough.

Handwashing

Washing Hands Song

Tune: Row, Row, Row Your Boat

Wash, wash, wash your hands,
Soap will make them clean!
Scrub the germs 'til they fall off,
They go down the drain.

Washing Hands Chant

Chant

Germs, germs, germs, I have germs on my hands.
Germs, I have germs on my hands – Icky!
Wash, wash, wash, I am washing my hands.
Wash, I am washing my hands. – Alright!
Scrub, scrub, scrub, I am scrubbing my hands.
Scrub, I am scrubbing my hands. –Yee-haw!
Rinse, rinse, rinse, I am rinsing my hands.
Rinse, I am rinsing my hands. – Yippee!
Dry, dry, dry, I am drying my hands.
Dry, I am drying my hands. – Oh yeah!

My Hands Are Dirty!

Tune: BINGO

My hands are dirty, yes they are! But I know what to do-o.
Wash, wash, wash my hands!
Wash, wash, wash my hands!
Wash, wash, wash my hands until they're good like new!
Now my hands are clean and dry and I'm so very happy!
Yes, yes, yes they're clean!
Yes, yes, yes they're clean!
Yes, yes, yes they're clean and I'm so very happy!

The More We Wash Our Hands

Tune: The More We Get Together

The more we wash our hands, our hands, our hands,
The more we wash our hands, the healthier we'll be!
For your friends are my friends
and my friends are your friends.
The more we wash our hands, the healthier we'll be!

Handwashing

It's Time to Wash Our Hands

Tune: If You're Happy and You Know It

It's time to wash our hands at the sink. *(clap, clap)*
It's time to wash our hands at the sink. *(clap, clap)*
We'll scrub them good and clean,
It's part of our routine.
It's time to wash our hands at the sink. *(clap, clap)*.

Are You Ready?

Tune: Are You Sleeping?

Are you ready?
Are you ready?
To clean hands! To clean hands!
Clean your hands just like we learned.
Just make sure you wait your turn.
Cleaning hands. Cleaning hands.

Handwashing

This Is the Way We Wash Our Hands

Tune: Here We 'Round the Mulberry Bush

This is the way we wash our hands,
wash our hands, wash our hands.
This is the way we wash our hands,
when we're at school.

This is the way we rinse our hands,
rinse our hands, rinse our hands.
This is the way we rinse our hands,
when we're at school.

This is the way we lather the soap,
lather the soap, lather the soap.
This is the way we lather the soap,
when we're at school.

This is the way we rinse the soap,
rinse the soap, rinse the soap.
This is the way we rinse the soap,
when we're at school.

This is the way we dry our hands,
dry our hands, dry our hands.
This is the way we dry our hands,
when we're at school.

Handwashing

Whistling Washing Hands Song

Tune: Whistle While You Work

Time to wash your hands! *(whistle)*
It's time to wash the germs away
and clean your dirty hands.
It's time to wash your hands! *(whistle)*
It won't take long when there's a song
To help you wash your hands.

Wash, Wash, Wash Your Hands

Tune: Skip to My Lou

Wash, wash, wash your hands.
Wash, wash, wash your hands.
Wash, wash, wash your hands.
Washing cleans the germs off!

Cleaning Hands Song

Tune: Apples and Bananas

I like to clean, clean, clean, clean my dirty hands.
I like to clean, clean, clean, clean my dirty hands.
I like to wash, wash, wash, wash my hands with soap.
I like to wash, wash, wash, wash my hands with soap.
I like to rinse, rinse, rinse, rinse my hands with water.
I like to rinse, rinse, rinse, rinse my hands with water.
I like to dry, dry, dry, dry my hands with towels.
I like to dry, dry, dry, dry my hands with towels.

Get Those Germs Off

Tune: Rain, Rain, Go Away

Wash, wash, wash your hands.
You can do it, yes you can.
Soap and water, wash and scrub.
Get those germs off, rub-a-dub-dub.

Handwashing

Wash Your Hands

Tune: This Old Man

Wash your hands.
Wash your hands.
Soap will make them clean again.
With a scrub, scrub, scrub,
You'll make them look brand new.
Don't forget your fingernails too.

We March Our Feet Right to the Sink

Tune: The Ants Go Marching

We march our feet right to the sink, hurrah, hurrah.
We march our feet right to the sink, hurrah, hurrah.
We march our feet right to the sink,
we'll wash our hands until they're clean.
And the germs go down the drain, the drain, the drain.
Boom! Boom! Boom!

(Repeat the song or end with Boom! Boom! Boom! Boom!)

Handwashing

Tops & Bottoms

Tune: Are You Sleeping?

Tops and bottoms, *(rub top and bottom of hands)*
Tops and bottoms, *(rub top and bottom of hands)*
In between, in between. *(rub fingers)*
Rinse your hands off really good, *(rinse hands off)*
Dry them, dry them like you should. *(dry them off)*
Clean, clean, clean. Clean, clean clean!

Soap Song

Tune: London Bridge Is Falling Down

Water washes dirt away,
Dirt away, dirt away.
Water washes dirt away,
Wash with water.
Soap will make my hands so clean,
Hands so clean, hands so clean.
Soap will make my hands so clean,
Scrub all over.
Rinsing makes the soap come off,
Soap come off, soap come off.
Rinsing makes the soap come off.
Now let's dry them!

Lining Up

A transition time that tends to be tricky is lining children up to go into the hall. There can be a lot of wasted time and unwanted behavior from children during this time. These songs will signal to students to line up quickly, give their attention to the teacher, and to walk quietly in the hall.

Lining Up

Finger On Your Lips

Tune: If You're Happy and You Know It

Put your finger on your lips, zip your lips. Shhh, shh!
Put your finger on your lips, zip your lips. Shhh shh!
Put your finger on your lips and do not let it slip.
Put your finger on your lips, zip your lips. Shhh shh!

Clapsies, Crazies

Chant

Clapsies, crazies,
Whoopsies, daisies, *(roll hands over head)*
High, low, *(reach high and then low)*
Heel, toe. *(touch heel to the floor, then toe of same foot)*
Don't you know? *(point to head)*
I'm ready to go! *(raise arms in running position)*

Lining Up

Ready for the Hall

Tune: Farmer in the Dell

Our hands are by our sides,
We're standing nice and tall,
Our lips are very quiet,
And we're ready for the hall.

The Quiet Chant

Chant

Hands on your hip.
Finger on your lip.
No sound at all
As we walk down the hall.

Lining Up

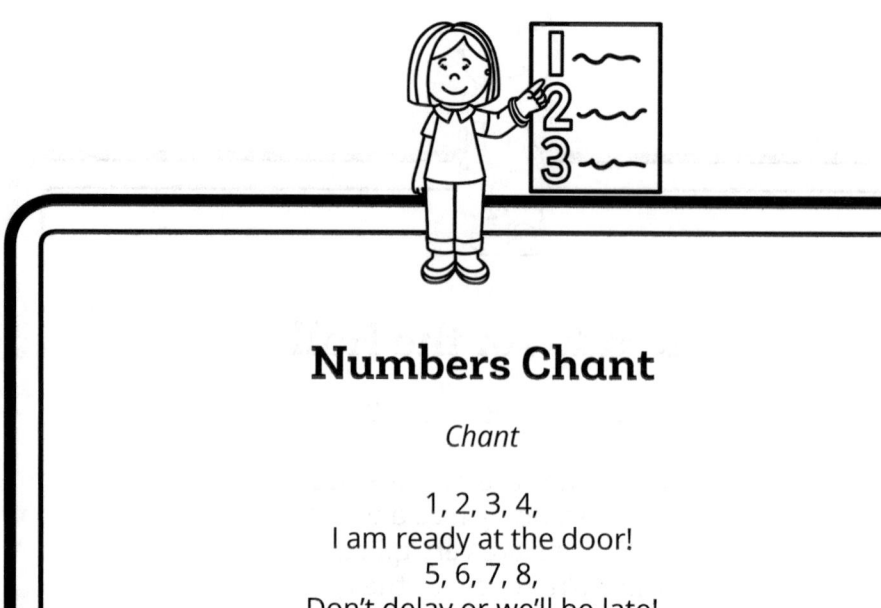

Numbers Chant

Chant

1, 2, 3, 4,
I am ready at the door!
5, 6, 7, 8,
Don't delay or we'll be late!

Show Me a Line

Chant

Show me a line, yes that would be fine!
Show me a line, by the time I count to 9.
1, 2, 3 - come make a line by me.
4, 5, 6 – you better hurry, quick!
7, 8, 9 – and now your line looks fine.

Line Up Chant

Chant

1, 2, listen and do.
3, 4, face the door.
5, 6, fingers on lips.
7, 8, line up straight.
9, 10, now the quiet walking begins.

No More Talking

Tune: Are You Sleeping?

Are you talking? Are you talking?
In the hall? In the hall?
No more talking, when we are out walking,
In the hall, in the hall.

Lining Up

Time to Stop

Chant

Lights off, time to stop!
Come up quickly – chop, chop!
A line we'll form, oh so straight.
And then quietly we wait.

Are You Ready for the Hall?

Tune: Do Your Ears Hang Low?

Are you ready for the hall?
Are you standing nice and tall?
Are your hands behind your back?
Are you leaving any gaps?
Are you quiet as can be?
Are you looking straight at me?
Now, let's walk quietly.

Lining Up

If You're Ready and You Know It

Tune: If You're Happy and You Know It

If you're ready and you know it, clap your hands. *(clap, clap)*
If you're ready and you know it, clap your hands. *(clap, clap)*
If you're ready and you know it, then I should see you show it.
If you're ready and you know it, clap your hands. *(clap, clap)*

When We Walk in the Hall

Tune: Mary Had a Little Lamb

When we walk, we don't talk,
We don't talk, we don't talk!
When we walk, we don't talk,
We listen to what's said!
When we walk, we're in a line,
In a line, in a line.
When we walk, we're in a line.
Our hands are by our sides!

Lining Up

Make a Line

Tune: Yankee Doodle

Time to line up at the door.
Please show me a straight line.
Hands by side, let's see your eyes,
It's time to make a line.
Make a line for the hall.
Make a line quickly.
Make a line for the hall.
Let's make it very quickly!

It's Time to Go!

Tune: Boom, Boom, Ain't It Great to Be Crazy?

Boom, boom!
It's time to go-o!
Boom, boom!
It's time to go-o!
Hurry up, make a line, mouths are shut!
Boom, boom!
It's time to...go-o!

I Spy Colors

Tune: Are You Sleeping?

I spy blue, I spy blue.
In the room, in the room!
Make your way up to the door.
But only if it's blue you wore.
I spy blue. I spy blue.

*(Continue the song with other colors
until all children have lined up.)*

Outside

It can be difficult to manage your class when they line up to go outdoors to play or to come back inside. Children have a lot of energy and singing a transition song helps to calm students down. It also helps line them up more quickly!

Outside

Going Outside

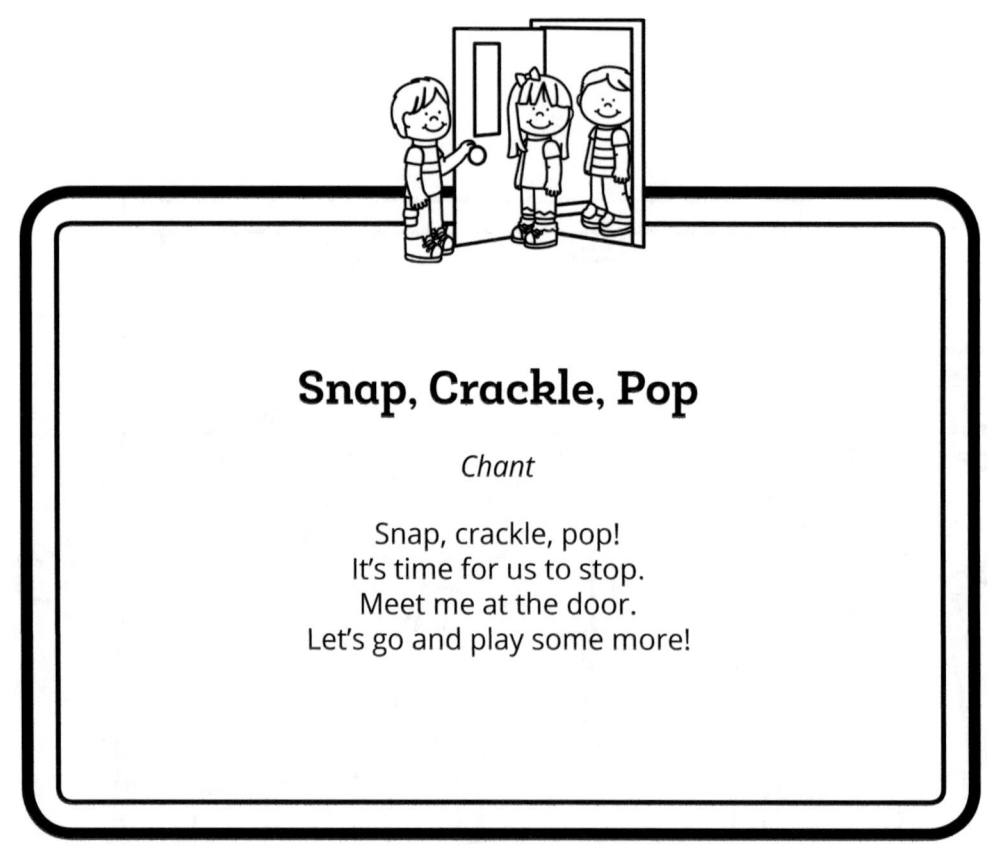

Snap, Crackle, Pop

Chant

Snap, crackle, pop!
It's time for us to stop.
Meet me at the door.
Let's go and play some more!

Look at the Clock

Tune: I'm a Little Teapot

Look at the clock,
It's time to play!
Let's go outside, it's a beautiful day.
When you get all lined up,
Here me say!
Open the doors, let's go and play!

Balance Rope Song

Tune: Twinkle, Twinkle Little Star

Set up: Place a rope on the ground and tell the kids you are walking on a bridge over lava and they have to balance and get to the other side without falling!

Balance, balance on this rope.
I walk upon this long tightrope.
I hope to make it to the end,
Then I'll run outside with friends!
You can do it! Walk with pride!
Try it and then go outside!

Let's Go Outside

Tune: Wheels on the Bus

Stop all your work, it's time to play.
Time to play, time to play!
Stop all your work, it's time to play.
Let's go outside!

I'm Ready for a Break to Play Outside

Tune: I'm a Little Teapot

I'm ready for a break to play outside.
We've worked so hard that I feel fried.
When we get all lined up at the door,
Just open the doors and hear me roar!

We Are Walking to the Door

Tune: It's a Small World

We are walking to the door.
We are walking to the door.
We are walking to the door.
It is time to play!

It's Time to Go Out

Tune: Boom, Boom, Ain't it Great to Be Crazy?

Boom, boom!
It's time to go out.
Boom, boom!
It's time to go out.
Put away, tidy up, go line up.
Boom, boom!
It's time to...go out!

Outside

Time to Go

Tune: Jingle Bells

Time to go!
Time to go!
Time to go outside!
We line up at the door so nice,
So we can go outside!
Time to go!
Time to go!
Time to go outside!
We can't wait to play with friends,
Let's go to play outside!

Outside

Coming Inside

Come Inside

Tune: Are You Sleeping?

Are you ready? Are you ready?
To go in, to go in!
We had fun playing,
Now it's time for learning.
Come inside. Come inside.

Inside Time

Tune: Do You Know the Muffin Man?

Do you know what time it is?
What time it is? What time it is?
Do you know what time it is?
It's time to go inside!

Are You Standing in a Line?

Tune: Do Your Ears Hang Low?

Are you standing in a line?
Are you looking mighty fine?
Are you keeping to yourself?
Are you quiet like a mouse?
Are you looking at the doors?
Are you ready for indoors?
It's time to go inside!

Are You Ready to Go Inside?

Tune: Finger Family Song

Are you ready? Are you ready?
To come inside.
Yes I am, Yes I am,
My hands are by my side.
Are you ready? Are you ready?
To be silent.
Yes I am, Yes I am,
I'm being very quiet.
Are you ready? Are you ready?
To go to class.
Yes I am, Yes I am,
Outside time has passed.

It's Time to Make a Line

Tune: Baa, Baa Black Sheep

Hello friends, it's time to make a line!
Yes, like that. You're looking very fine.
Hands by your hips.
Fingers on your lips.
Look right at me.
I'm counting – 1, 2, 3!
Let's make a line, it's time to inside!
Walk quietly, your hands are by your side.

Outside

Our Feet Go Marching

Tune: The Ants Go Marching

Our feet go marching one by one, hurrah, hurrah.
Our feet go marching one by one, hurrah, hurrah.
We had so much fun in the sun,
but now our playtime is over and done.
So our feet go marching down…the hall…
to go to…our rooms.
Boom, Boom, Boom, BOOM!

If You're Ready to Go In

Tune: If You're Happy and You Know It

If you're ready to go in, clap with me! *(clap, clap)*
If you're ready to go in, clap with me! *(clap, clap)*
If you're ready to go in, then let's see your biggest grin.
If you're ready to go in, clap with me! *(clap, clap)*

Cleaning Up

Cleaning up time is not typically a favorite activity for preschoolers. This time of day can also be noisy and chaotic. Having a chant or song to sing helps the task of cleaning become less daunting and makes the time go by more quickly!

Cleaning Up

We're Putting Our Toys Away

Tune: The Farmer in the Dell

We're putting our toys away,
We hope it won't take all day!
To have more fun, we'll get it all done.
We're putting our toys away.

Tidy Up

Tune: Jingle Bells

Tidy up, tidy up, put the toys away.
Tidy up, tidy up, we're finished for today.
Tidy up, tidy up, put the toys away.
For we'll get them out again the next time that we play.

Clean Up Chant

Chant

I turn off the lights.
I clap my hands.
Means clean-up time,
Throughout the land!

Twinkle Clean Up Song

Tune: Twinkle, Twinkle Little Star

Twinkle, twinkle, little star,
Stop and clean up where you are!
Time to put your things away,
We clean up at the end of the day.
Twinkle, twinkle, little star,
Stop and clean up where you are!

Cleaning Up

Time to Stop

Chant

Tootsie roll, *(roll hands)*
Lollipop. *(pretend to lick lollipop)*
We've been working, but now let's stop.
(hold hands out like a stop sign)
Put away and tidy up.
Then it's time to go line up!

It's Clean-Up Time

Tune: Head, Shoulders, Knees and Toes

Stop and freeze,
It's clean-up time, clean-up time.
Stop and freeze,
It's clean-up time, clean-up time.
Clean your space,
Let's tidy up this place.
Stop and freeze,
It's clean-up time, clean-up time.

Cleaning Up

Heigh-ho, Heigh-ho

Tune: Heigh-ho, Heigh-ho

Heigh-ho, heigh-ho,
It's clean up time you know.
Put the toys away for another day,
Heigh-ho, heigh-ho!

Where Has the Time Gone?

Tune: Oh Where, Oh Where Has My Little Dog Gone?

Oh where, oh where has the time gone today?
It's time to clean up the room!
Put your things away and tidy your space.
It's time to clean up the room!

Cleaning Up

I Like to Clean Up

Tune: La Cucaracha

I like to clean up.
I like to clean up.
Clean up, pick up, put away!
I like to clean up.
I like to clean up.
Clean up happens every day!

Clap, Clap! It's Time to Clean Up!

Tune: Boom Boom Ain't It Great to Be Crazy?

Clap, clap! Now it's time to clean up!
Clap, clap! Now it's time to clean up!
Put away, tidy up, clean your space.
Clap, clap! Now it's time to...clean up!

Clean Up Chant

Chant

1, 2, 3, 4,
Clean-up time starts on the floor!
5, 6, 7, 8,
Don't delay or we'll be late!

Stop and Freeze

Tune: This Old Man

Stop and freeze.
Look at me!
Time to clean up, zip-a-dee-dee!
With a quick pick up,
We'll make the room like new!
Let's start cleaning 'round the room.

Cleaning Up

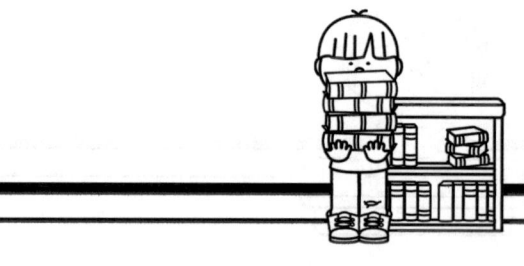

I Clean Up When the Day Is Done

Tune: Mary Had a Little Lamb

Clean up when the day is done,
Day is done, day is done!
Clean up when the day is done,
It's time to go!

Are You Ready to Clean Up?

Tune: Finger Family Song

Are you ready? Are you ready?
To clean up!
Yes we are, yes we are.
Ready to clean up!

Clean-Up Song with Tongs

Chant

Set up: Place tongs on the ground and have students pick up the toys using tongs.
This makes clean up time more of a game!

Chant

Grab a tong! *(teacher)*
Grab a tong! *(student)*
And sing this song! *(teacher)*
And sing this song! *(student)*

Tune: Mary Had a Little Lamb

I can pick up toys with tongs,
Toys with tongs, toys with tongs!
I can pick up toys with tongs,
It never takes us long!
Make the room nice and neat,
Nice and clean, nice and neat.
Make the room nice and neat,
Then let's take a seat!

Brain Breaks

It's vital to use play brain breaks throughout the day with your preschoolers. These types of songs and chants are used to activate, energize, and stimulate a child's brain. When you incorporate brain breaks into your day, this helps improve a child's ability to concentrate when you go back to classroom work. Research shows that children should have some sort of brain break every 25-30 minutes. These next 30 transitions will give you ideas for brain break times. This section is broken up into three types of brain breaks: action breaks, crossing the midline exercises, and finger plays.

Brain Breaks

Action Breaks

Action breaks incorporate physical activity into your day. These 10 songs and chants are designed to get your students to move their bodies in order to increase blood flow and oxygen to the brain. Brain breaks will lead to improved concentration when it's time to sit back down in the classroom.

Action Break Song

Tune: Here We Go 'Round the Mulberry Bush

This is the way I like to jump, like to jump, like to jump.
This is the way I like to jump, off to _____. *(next action)*

*Action: dance, march, hop, crawl, run, flap elbows.

Ending: Now the song is done!

Exercise Chant

Chant

Exercise, exercise!
Let's see you exercise!
Stretch high!
Stretch low!
Let's see how *(child's name)* exercise will go.

(Have the child demonstrate an exercise for others to follow.)

Rickety Tickity

Chant

Rickety, tickity look at me! *(hands behind your back)*
How many fingers do you see?
(hold fingers up and students count them)
Rickety, tickity look at me!
Now do that many *(action)* with me!

(Action: jumps, push-ups, high-fives, spins, etc.)

Brain Breaks

If You're Happy and You Know It Action Song

Tune: If You're Happy and You Know It

If you're happy and you know it, hop with a smile.
If you're happy and you know it, hop with a smile.
If you're happy and you know it,
then your face will surely show it.
If you're happy and you know it, hop with a smile!

Variations:

If you're sad and you know it, walk with a frown.

If you're mad and you know it, stomp your feet!

If you're excited and you know it, jump up and down!

If you're scared and you know it, hide your eyes.

If you're silly and you know it, wiggle your hips!

If you're tired and you know it, lay on the ground.

I'll Find a Friend

Tune: Farmer in the Dell

(child holds hands with another child)
I'll find a friend at school.
I'll find a friend at school.
I'm so glad I came today,
I'll find a friend at school.

(skip around the room)
We'll skip around the room.
We'll skip around the room.
I'm so glad I came today,
We'll skip around the room!

(jump around the room)
We'll jump around the room.
We'll jump around the room.
I'm so glad I came today,
We'll jump around the room!

(clap hands around the room)
We'll clap around the room.
We'll clap around the room.
I'm so glad I came today,
We'll clap around the room!

(give friends a hug)
We'll give our friends a hug.
We'll give our friends a hug.
I'm so glad I came today,
We'll give our friends a hug!

Brain Breaks

The Egg Song

Tune: La Cucaracha

Shake your eeeggg!
Shake your eeeggg!
Shake it, shake it all around.
Shake your eeeggg!
Shake your eeeggg!
Now let's take it to the ground.
Roll your eeeggg!
Roll your eeeggg!
Roll it, roll it all around.
Roll your eeeggg!
Roll your eeeggg!
Go and pick up off the ground.
Shake it faaast!
Shake it faaast!
Shake it, shake it very fast.
Shake it faaast!
Shake it faaast!
Shaking fast is a blast!
Shake it sloooow!
Shake it sloooow!
Shake it, shake it very slow.
Shake it sloooow!
Shake it sloooow!
Now get ready to throw!
Toss your eeeggg!
Toss your eeeggg!
Toss it gently in the air.
Toss your eeeggg!
Toss your eeeggg!
Now go set it over there.

(Have a basket for kids to set their eggs in.)

Brain Breaks

The Color Song

Tune: If You're Happy and You Know It

If your clothes have any red, any red.
If your clothes have any red, any red.
If your clothes have any red, put your finger on your head.
If your clothes have any red, any red.

Variations:
Blue – finger on your shoe
Yellow – smile like a happy fellow
Brown- turn your smile into a frown
Black – put your hands behind your back
White – stomp your feet with all your might

This Is the Way I Move!

Tune: Here We Go 'Round the Mulberry Bush

This is the way I touch my nose,
Touch my nose, touch my nose.
This is the way I touch my nose, when I'm at school!

Variations: jump up and down, spin around,
`hop in the air, stretch up high,
bend to the floor, balance on one foot, spin in a circle

Brain Breaks

I Like to Move

Tune: Skip to My Lou

Hey, hey! I like to move!
Hey, hey! I like to move!
Hey, hey! I like to move!
Watch me move my body.

Swing with my partner,
Two-da-la-do!
Swing with my partner,
Two-da-la-do!
Swing with my partner,
Two-da-la-do!
I can swing with my partner.

Jump up and down, Yippee yi yay!
Jump up and down, Yippee yi yay!
Jump up and down, Yippee yi yay!
I can jump up and down.

Spin to my right, Oooh ahhh oooh!
Spin to my left, Oooh ahhh oooh!
Spin to my right, Oooh ahhh ooh!
I can spin in a circle.

Shake a friend's hand, How do you do?
Shake a friend's hand, How do you do?
Shake a friend's hand, How do you do?
I can shake lots of hands.

I Can Move!

Tune: Baby Shark

I can clap! *(doo, doo...doo, doo, doo, doo!)*
I can clap! *(doo, doo...doo, doo, doo, doo!)*
I can clap! *(doo, doo...doo, doo, doo, doo!)*
I can clap!

I can jump! *(doo, doo...doo, doo, doo, doo!)*
I can jump! *(doo, doo...doo, doo, doo, doo!)*
I can jump! *(doo, doo...doo, doo, doo, doo!)*
I can jump!

I can run! *(doo, doo...doo, doo, doo, doo!)*
I can run! *(doo, doo...doo, doo, doo, doo!)*
I can run! *(doo, doo...doo, doo, doo, doo!)*
I can run!

Variations: skip, hop, balance, spin, twist

Brain Breaks

Movement Freeze Song

Tune: Do You Know the Muffin Man?

Do you like to jump around?
Jump around? Jump around?
Do you like to jump around?
Jump and now let's freeze.
(freeze until you hear the next action)

Do you like to roll around?
Roll around? Roll around?
Do you like to roll around?
Roll and now let's freeze.

Do you like to throw a ball?
Throw a ball? Throw a ball?
Do you like to throw a ball?
Throw and now let's freeze.

Do you like to tiptoe walk?
Tiptoe walk? Tiptoe walk?
Do you like to tiptoe walk?
Tiptoe, now let's freeze.

Do you like to crawl around?
Crawl around? Crawl around?
Do you like to crawl around?
Crawl and now let's freeze.

Brain Breaks

Crossing the Midline

Crossing the midline exercises help build connections in our brain. The body's midline is an imaginary line down the center of the body that divides the body into left and right. Every time you cross that line with either side of your body, you are crossing midline. This skill is a very important part of a child's development and leads to the ability to do school activities such as reading, writing, and play activities. These 10 songs and chants use actions or props and are focused on exercises crossing the midline.

Give Yourself a Hug

Tune: Hokey Pokey

You put your right hand out,
You cross it to your shoulder.
You put your left hand out,
And you cross it to your shoulder.
You give yourself a hug,
And you wiggle all over.
Let's give yourself a hug! *(clap, clap)*

79

Let's Make an 8

Tune: Down By the Bay

*Use scarves to make a figure 8 in the air
Let's make an 8.
Oh, it's so great!
Let's make an 8.
Oh, it's so great!
Let's make an 8.
Oh, it's so great!
Did you know that this helps my brain communicate?
Let's make an 8!

Midline Chant

Chant

1, 2, punch with me.
(punch one arm across to the other side then do the other arm)
3, 4, scoop the floor. *(make a scooping motion to the floor)*
5, 6, shake your hips. *(move your hips around)*
7, 8, make an eight. *(draw an 8 in the air with your finger)*
9, 10, let's do it again!

(Alternative ending: and that's the end!)

The Passing Song

Tune: Here We Go 'Round the Mulberry Bush

*children sit with their backs together
and one child holds a ball.
Pass the ball by twisting body to hand it to the other child.

Around, around the ball goes around.
I pass the ball to my friend.
I keep on going 'til I hear,
"Stop!" from my teacher.

Pat-a-Cake Break

Chant

Pat-a-cake, pat-a-cake
Let's take a break.
Pat-a-cake, pat-a-cake
It's a piece of cake!
(do the pat-a-cake motions with a partner)

This Is the Way

Tune: Here We Go 'Round the Mulberry Bush

This is the way we wash the car,
Wash the car, wash the car.
This is the way we wash the car,
When we clean our car.
(do big washing movements with both hands)

This is the way we shovel the sand,
Shovel the sand, shovel the sand.
This is the way we shovel the sand,
When we play at the beach.
(pretend to scoop sand from one side of the body and place it in a bucket on the opposite side of the body)

This is the way we fly a kite,
Fly a kite, fly a kite.
This is the way we fly a kite,
When we play at the park.
(pretend to fly a kite with big arm movements)

This is the way we swim in the pool,
Swim in the pool, swim in the pool.
This is the way we swim at the pool,
On a hot summer day.
(do swimming motions with your arms)

Pat-a-Cake Wiggle

Tune: Pat-a-Cake

Pat-a-cake, pat-a-cake, let's play a game.
Have your partner do the same.
Clap right, clap left, then clap in the middle.
Then stop what you're doing and do a little wiggle!

(Do the song in different speeds: very fast or very slow.)

Crawling Song

Tune: The Ants Go Marching

We crawl across the floor on our knees, our knees.
We crawl across the floor on our knees, our knees.
We crawl on the floor to move our body.
We make sure we don't run into somebody.
And we all crawl 'til this song is done,
Is done, is done.
Boom, boom, boom BOOM!

Brain Breaks

Climbing Ladder Chant

Chant

(Have children do a climbing ladder motion while chanting.)

Climbing, climbing,
Up we go!
Don't stop climbing,
Stay with the flow!

Let's keep going,
Just a little bit more.
Oh we're getting near,
I can see it over there.

Climbing, climbing
Up we go!
Don't stop climbing,
Keep with the flow!

Look we're at the top!
Whew! Now it's time for us to stop.

If You Like to Move Your Body

Tune: If You're Happy and You Know It

(draw an 8 in the air with your finger)
If you like to move your body, make an 8.
If you like to move your body, make an 8.
If you like to move your body, let me see you make an 8
If you like to move your body, make an 8.

(twist your body)
If you like to move your body, do the twist.
If you like to move your body, do the twist.
If you like to move your body, let me see you do the twist.
If you like to move your body, do the twist.

(tap your hand to the opposite elbow)
If you like to move your body, tap your elbows.
If you like to move your body, tap your elbows.
If you like to move your body,
let me see you tap your elbows.
If you like to move your body, tap your elbows.

(crawl on the floor)
If you like to move your body, crawl around.
If you like to move your body, crawl around.
If you like to move your body, let me see you crawl around.
If you like to move your body, crawl around.

Brain Breaks

Finger Plays

Finger plays are rhymes and songs that use actions with finger movements. These kinds of transitions have less actions, but use hands or fingers to illustrate the story. Children develop memory and recall skills as they sing these songs. These kinds of rhymes are wonderful for focusing children's attention or just to entertain them during a break in the day.

10 Little Chicks

Chant

Five eggs and five eggs, *(hold up 10 fingers)*
That makes 10.
Sitting on top is the mother hen.
(cover one hand with the other)
Crack, crack, crack.
(clap three times)
What do I see?
10 little chicks,
As cute as can be! *(hold up 10 fingers)*

Kites

Chant

*Hold up fingers for this chant and move them around like kites

One little kite, up in the blue.
(hold one finger up)

Along came another, then there were two.
(hold two fingers up)

Two little kites, over the tree.
Along came another, then there were three.
(hold three fingers up)

Three little kites, watch them soar.
Along came another, then there were four.
(hold four fingers up)

Four little kites, they act so alive.
Next came the last one, and then there were five!
(hold five fingers up)

Brain Breaks

Hippity-Hop, Hippity-Hay

Chant

(Hold up five fingers and take a finger away for each verse.)

Hippity-hop, hippity-hay,
Five little bunnies went out to play.
Hippity-hop, hippity-hay,
One little bunny hopped away.

Hippity-hop, hippity-hay,
Four little bunnies went out to play.
Hippity-hop, hippity-hay,
One little bunny hopped away.

Hippity-hop, hippity-hay,
Three little bunnies went out to play.
Hippity-hop, hippity-hay,
One little bunny hopped away.

Hippity-hop, hippity-hay,
Two little bunnies went out to play.
Hippity-hop, hippity-hay,
One little bunny hopped away.

Hippity-hop, hippity-hay,
One little bunny went out to play.
Hippity-hop, hippity-hay,
One little bunny hopped away.

Hippity-hop, hippity-hay,
No more bunnies are playing today.
Hippity-hop, hippity-hay,
I hope they come back another day!

Brain Breaks

Five Little Chicks

Chant

Five little chicks went walking one day,
(hold up five fingers)
Into the barn and around the hay.
(change fingers to walking motion)
Mother hen said, "Cluck, cluck, cluck, CLACK!"
And four little chicks came wandering back.

Four little chicks went walking one day,
(hold up four fingers)
Into the barn and around the hay.
(change fingers to walking motion)
Mother hen said, "Cluck, cluck, cluck, CLACK!"
And three little chicks came wandering back.

Three little chicks went walking one day,
(hold up three fingers)
Into the barn and around the hay.
(change fingers to walking motion)
Mother hen said, "Cluck, cluck, cluck, CLACK!"
And two little chicks came wandering back.

Two little chicks went walking one day,
(hold up two fingers)
Into the barn and around the hay.
(change fingers to walking motion)
Mother hen said, "Cluck, cluck, cluck, CLACK!"
And one little chick came wandering back.

One little chick went walking one day,
(hold up one finger)
Into the barn and around the hay.
(change fingers to walking motion)
Mother hen said, "Cluck, cluck, cluck, CLACK!"
And all five little chicks came wandering back.

Five Little Ladybugs

Tune: 5 Little Monkeys Swinging in a Tree

(hold five fingers up to represent the ladybugs)
Five little ladybugs sitting on a leaf,
Soaking in the sunshine and the soft, warm breeze.
Along came Mr. Bird, as quiet as can be,
And snatched that ladybug off of the leaf!

(hold four fingers up to represent the ladybugs)
Four little ladybugs sitting on a leaf,
Soaking in the sunshine and the soft, warm breeze.
Along came Mr. Bird, as quiet as can be,
And snatched that ladybug off of the leaf!

(hold three fingers up to represent the ladybugs)
Three little ladybugs sitting on a leaf,
Soaking in the sunshine and the soft, warm breeze.
Along came Mr. Bird, as quiet as can be,
And snatched that ladybug off of the leaf!

(hold two fingers up to represent the ladybugs)
Two little ladybugs sitting on a leaf,
Soaking in the sunshine and the soft, warm breeze.
Along came Mr. Bird, as quiet as can be,
And snatched that ladybug off of the leaf!

(hold one finger up to represent the ladybugs)
One little ladybug sitting on a leaf,
Soaking in the sunshine and the soft, warm breeze.
Along came Mr. Bird, as quiet as can be,
And snatched that ladybug off of the leaf!

No little ladybugs sitting on a leaf,
They all have gone away from the soft, warm breeze.
But along came Mr. Bird, as quiet as can be,
And he dropped all the ladybugs back on the leaf!
(hold five fingers back up to represent the ladybugs)

Wiggly Worms

Chant

You have 10 wiggly worms
(hold 10 fingers up)
Who are as wiggly as can be.
Help them get the wiggles out
Let's do it...1, 2, 3!
(hold 10 fingers up and wiggle them around)

Wiggle them up and wiggle them down,
Wiggle your worms around and around.
Wiggle them high and wiggle them low,
Wiggle them fast and wiggle them slow.
Wiggle them by your toes,
Wiggle them on your nose.

Now the wiggles are gone,
And the worms let out a big yawn.
Go put the worms to bed,
And lay down your sleepy head.
(place your palms together and lay them in your lap)

My Red Balloon

Chant

I have a red balloon,
It's as big as it can be!
(hold your hands out like you have a large balloon)
I throw it in the air, *(tossing motion in the air)*
and watch it fall on me. *(slowly bring hands down)*
I toss it to the ground, *(throw motion to the ground)*
and then it bounces around. *(bouncing motion with hands)*
Pop! What's that sound? *(shrug your shoulders)*
My balloon's no longer round.
*(hold your hands together like
you're holding a popped balloon)*

Fireflies in the Sky

Tune: Twinkle, Twinkle Little Star

(Twinkle all 10 fingers to look like fireflies.)

Fireflies up in the sky!
Twinkling, twinkling in the night.
1, 2, 3, 4, 5, 6, 7,
8, 9, 10, they fly toward heaven!
(count the fingers then do a flying motion toward haven)
Fireflies up in the sky!
Twinkling, twinkling in the night.

Baby Birds

Chant

One baby bird, lonely and brand new.
(hold one finger up)
Finds a new friend, and then there are two.
(hold two fingers up)
Two baby birds, sitting on the tree.
They find another bird, and then there are three.
(hold three fingers up)
Three baby birds, looking for some more.
They find another bird, and then there are four.
(hold four fingers up)
Four baby birds, starting to really thrive,
Up comes another, and then there are five!
(hold five fingers up)

Fireflies

Tune: 10 Little Indians

(Hold up one finger at a time until you have 10.)

At the end move all 10 fingers with the word "glowing."
One little, two little, three little fireflies,
Four little, five little, six little fireflies,
Seven little, eight little, nine little fireflies,
10 little fireflies…glowing!

Building Character

These 10 songs focus on building good character in children. They focus on the areas of showing respect, being gentle, having patience, sharing, being trustworthy, showing kindness, and making good choices. These songs are reminder to students of the expectations in the classroom and also serve to promote a positive environment in the classroom.

Building Character

Building Patience

Tune: Mary Had a Little Lamb

Building patience as we wait,
As we wait, as we wait.
Building patience as we wait,
Let's show patience.

Making Good Choices Song

Tune: Boom, Boom, Ain't It Great to Be Crazy?

Boom, boom. I am making good choices!
Boom, boom. I am making good choices!
Being a leader, all day long.
Boom, boom. I am making good choices.

Building Character

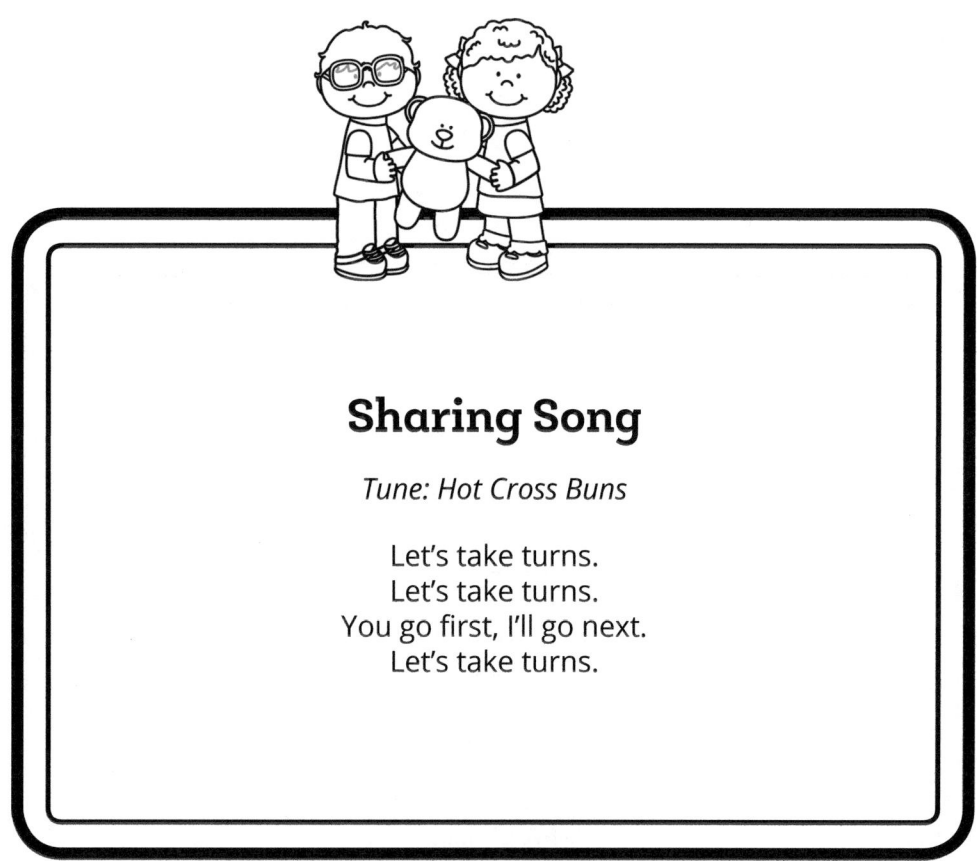

Sharing Song

Tune: Hot Cross Buns

Let's take turns.
Let's take turns.
You go first, I'll go next.
Let's take turns.

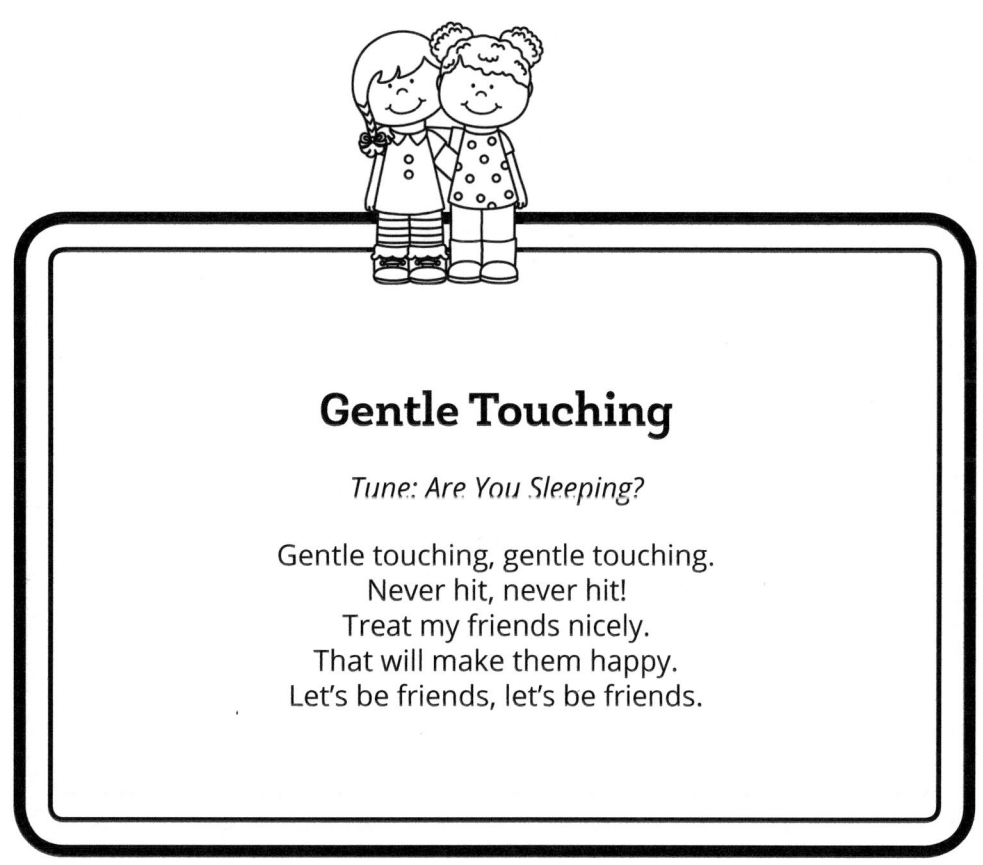

Gentle Touching

Tune: Are You Sleeping?

Gentle touching, gentle touching.
Never hit, never hit!
Treat my friends nicely.
That will make them happy.
Let's be friends, let's be friends.

The Kind Song

Tune: BINGO

I smile at my friends at school,
Because it shows them kindness!

Chorus:

K-I-N-D, kind!
K-I-N-D, kind!
K-I-N-D, kind!
Kindness makes us happy!

I care for others in my class,
Because it shows them kindness!

(chorus)

I am polite with words I say,
Because it shows them kindness!

(chorus)

I share my toys with all my friends,
Because it shows them kindness!

(chorus)

I hold the door open for friends,
Because it shows them kindness!

(chorus)

Building Character

Let Me See You Show It

Tune: If You're Happy and You Know It

If you're making a good choice,
  clap your hands! *(clap, clap)*
If you're making a good choice,
  clap your hands! *(clap, clap)*
If you're making a good choice,
  then I should see you show it.
If you're making a good choice,
  clap your hands! *(clap, clap)*

If you're showing that you're brave,
  clap your hands! *(clap, clap)*
If you're showing that you're brave,
  clap your hands! *(clap, clap)*
If you're showing that you're brave,
  then I should see you show it.
If you're showing that you're brave,
  clap your hands! *(clap, clap)*

If you're being kind and caring,
  clap your hands! *(clap, clap)*
If you're being kind and caring,
  clap your hands! *(clap, clap)*
If you're being kind and caring,
  then I should see you show it.
If you're being kind and caring,
  clap your hands! *(clap, clap)*

If you're helping friends around you,
  clap your hands! *(clap, clap)*
If you're helping friends around you,
  clap your hands! *(clap, clap)*
If you're helping friends around you,
  then I should see you show it.
If you're helping friends around you,
  clap your hands! *(clap, clap)*

Building Character

Showing Good Character

Tune: London Bridge Is Falling Down

Show respect to all my friends,
All my friends, all my friends.
Show respect to all my friends,
That shows kindness.

Try new things out when I'm scared,
When I'm scared, when I'm scared.
Try new things out when I'm scared.
That shows courage.

Tell the truth no matter what,
No matter what, no matter what.
Tell the truth no matter what,
That shows honesty.

Taking turns and being nice,
Being nice, being nice.
Taking turns and being nice,
That shows fairness.

Building Character

I Can See

Tune: Do You Know the Muffin Man?

*During the song, students can point to
a friend who shows that characteristic.

I can see a friend that's brave,
A friend that's brave, a friend that's brave.
I can see a friend that's brave, that's making a good choice.

I can see a friend who shares,
A friend who shares, a friend who shares.
I can see a friend who shares, that's making a good choice.

I can see a friend I trust,
A friend I trust, a friend I trust.
I can see a friend I trust, that's making a good choice.

I can see a friend who cares,
A friend who cares, a friend who cares.
I can see a friend who cares, that's making a good choice.

Building Character

The More I Make Good Choices

Tune: The More We Get Together

The more I make good choices, good choices, good choices.
The more I make good choices, the happier I'll be.
By sharing and helping, respecting and caring.
The more I make good choices, the happier I'll be.

Trustworthy Song

Tune: Twinkle, Twinkle Little Star

I can show I'm trustworthy,
Tell the truth— that's honesty.
Courage to do right, not wrong.
Being loyal all along.
I can show I'm trustworthy,
Make good choices, yes you'll see!

End of Day

This last set of songs are transitions to end the preschool day. Singing songs and rhymes are a great way to bring order to a chaotic time of the day and also add closure to day. Sending off the students with a song is a cheerful way to say goodbye!

End of Day

This Is the Way We Say Goodbye

Tune: Here We Go 'Round the Mulberry Bush

This is the way we say goodbye,
Say goodbye, say goodbye.
This is the way we say goodbye,
At school every day.
We give our friends a big high-five,
Big high-five, big high-five.
We give our a friends a big high-five,
When we say goodbye!

Goodbye Song

Tune: Hot Cross Buns

Let's say goodbye.
Let's say goodbye.
To our friends.
To our friends.
Let's say goodbye.
(wave hands during the song)

End of Day

Hurry Up

Chant

1, 2, 3, 4,
Everybody face the door.
5, 6, 7, 8,
Hurry up or we'll be late!

It's Time to Say Goodbye

Tune: If You're Happy and You Know It

It's time to say goodbye to all my friends. *(clap, clap)*
It's time to say goodbye to all my friends. *(clap, clap)*
It's time to say goodbye, show a smile and wink an eye.
It's time to say goodbye to all my friends. *(clap, clap)*

End of Day

Who Is Ready?

Tune: The Bear Went Over the Mountain

(child's name) is ready.
(child's name) is ready.
(child's name) is ready.
To go back home today!

Goodbye Friends

Tune: Twinkle, Twinkle, Little Star

Goodbye, goodbye all my friends,
Learning time has come to an end.
We played hard and had our fun.
We said goodbye, the day is done.
Goodbye, goodbye all my friends,
Learning time has come to an end.

End of Day

Are You Ready?

Tune: Are You Sleeping?

Are you ready?
Are you ready?
To go home! To go home!
We had fun together,
Playing with each other.
Goodbye friends, goodbye friends.

Our Day Is Done

Tune: Mary Had a Little Lamb

All day long we worked so hard,
Worked so hard, worked so hard!
All day long we worked so hard,
But now it's time to go!
Say goodbye to all our friends,
All our friends, all our friends!
Say goodbye to all our friends,
Because it's time to go!

End of Day

It's Time for Us to Go

Tune: Heigh-Ho! Heigh-Ho!

Heigh-ho! Heigh-ho!
It's time for us to go!
Put your things away,
It's the end of the day.
Heigh-ho! Heigh-ho!

It's Time to End Our Day

Tune: The Farmer and the Dell

It's time to end our day.
It's time to end our day.
It's time to say a big hooray,
And then be on our way!

End of Day

Quiet Goodbye Chant

Chant

Pea-nut butter, bread, and jam.
Let's say goodbye as quiet as we can.
Goodbye!

Waving Goodbye to My Friends

Tune: London Bridge is Falling Down

Waving goodbye to my friends,
To my friends, to my friends.
Waving goodbye to my friends,
See you all later!
(children wave goodbye to their friends during the song)

End of Day

It's Time to Stop and Go

Tune: A-Hunting We Will Go

It's time to stop and go.
It's time to stop and go.
Heigh-ho, the derry-o,
It's time to stop and go.

Time to Clean Up and Go Home

Tune: Head, Shoulders, Knees and Toes

Time to clean up and go home. *(clap, clap)*
Time to clean up and go home. *(clap, clap)*
Wave goodbye to your friends,
Learning time has come to an end.
Time to clean up and go home. *(clap, clap)*

End of Day

Oh It's Time to Say Goodbye to All My Friends

Tune: She'll Be Coming Around the Mountain

Oh it's time to say goodbye to all my friends! *(clap, clap)*
Oh it's time to say goodbye to all my friends! *(clap, clap)*
Swing your partner round and round.
(link arms with a friend and swing around)
Line up without making sounds. *(start to line up)*
Oh it's time to say goodbye to all my friends!
(shout) Goodbye!

About the Author

Angela is a mom to three boys, wife to an amazing man, lover of the Midwest, and daughter of a loving God. She is a writer and creator of TeachingMama.org, where she shares hands-on learning activities for young children. Angela is the author of *The Toddler Journey* and *The Preschool Journey*. She has a passion for music and loves to come up with rhymes and songs for pre-schoolers. Angela is a former teacher and has over 17 years of experience working with children.

You can connect with her on
Facebook, Twitter, Instagram, and Pinterest.

Made in the USA
Thornton, CO
05/27/23 22:22:52

0dd32db2-9463-46f5-ba20-1a8c35604452R01